THE AFRICAN WAR

Julius Caesar

Translated: William Alexander McDevitte
Edited by: D.P. Curtin

Dalcassian
Publishing
Company
PHILADELPHIA, PA

Library of Congress Cataloging-in-Publication Data

Copyright © 2019 Dalcassian Publishing Co.
In association with St. Macartan Press
All rights reserved.

1

Caesar, advancing by moderate journeys, and continuing his march without intermission, arrived at Lilybaeum, on the 14th day before the calends of January. Designing to embark immediately, though he had only one legion of new levies, and not quite six hundred horse, he ordered his tent to be pitched so near the sea-side that the waves lashed the very foot of it. This he did with a view that none should think he had time to delay, and that his men might be kept in readiness at a day or an hour's warning. Though the wind at that time was contrary, he nevertheless detained the soldiers and mariners on board, that he might lose no opportunity of sailing; the rather, because the forces of the enemy were announced by the inhabitants of the province, to consist of innumerable cavalry not to be numbered; four legions headed by Juba, together with a great body of light-armed troops; ten legions under the command of Scipio; a hundred and twenty elephants, and fleets in abundance. Yet he was not alarmed, nor lost his confident hopes and spirits. Meantime the number of galleys and transports increased daily; the new-levied legions flocked in to him from all parts; among the rest the fifth, a veteran legion, and about two thousand horse.

2

Having got together six legions and about two thousand horse, he embarked the legions as fast as they arrived, in the galleys, and the cavalry in the transports. Then sending the greatest part of the fleet before, with orders to sail for the island of Aponiana, not far from Lilybaeum; he himself continued a little longer in Sicily, and exposed to public sale some confiscated estates. Leaving all other affairs to the care of Allienus the praetor, who then commanded in the island; and strictly charging him to use the utmost expedition in embarking the remainder of the troops; he set sail the sixth day before the calends of January, and soon came up with the rest of the fleet. As the wind was favorable, and afforded a quick passage, he arrived the fourth day within sight of Africa, attended by a few galleys: for the transports, being mostly dispersed and scattered by the winds, with the exception of a few were driven different ways. Passing Clupea and Neapolis with the fleet, he continued for some time to coast along the shore, leaving many towns and castles behind him.

3

After he came before Adrumetum, where the enemy had a garrison, commanded by C. Considius, and where Cn. Piso appeared upon the shore toward Clupea, with the cavalry of Adrumetum, and about three thousand Moors, he stopped awhile, facing the port, till the rest of the fleet should come up, and then landed his men, though their number at that time did not exceed three thousand foot and a hundred and fifty horse. There, encamping before the town, he continued quiet, without offering any act of hostility, and restrained all from plunder. Meantime the inhabitants manned the walls, and assembled in great numbers before the gate, to defend themselves, their garrison within amounting to two legions. Caesar, having ridden round the town, and thoroughly examined its situation, returned to his camp. Some blamed his conduct on this occasion, and charged him with a considerable oversight, in not appointing a place of meeting to the pilots and captains of the fleet, or delivering them sealed instructions, according to his usual custom; which being opened at a certain time, might have directed them to assemble at a specified place. But in this Caesar acted not without design; for as he knew of no port in Africa that was clear of the enemy's forces, and where the fleet might rendezvous in security, he chose to rely entirely upon fortune, and land where occasion offered.

4

In the mean time, L. Plancus, one of Caesar's lieutenants, desired leave to treat with Considius, and try, if possible, to bring him to reason. Leave being granted accordingly, he wrote him a letter, and sent it into the town by a captive. When the captive arrived, and presented the letter, Considius, before he received it, demanded whence it came, and being told from Caesar, the Roman general, answered, "That he knew no general of the Roman forces but Scipio." Then, commending the messenger to be immediately slain in his presence, he delivered the letter, unread and unopened, to a trusty partisan, with orders to carry it directly to Scipio.

5

Caesar had now continued a day and a night before the town, without receiving any answer from Considius; the rest of the forces were not yet arrived; his cavalry was not considerable; he had not sufficient troops with him to invest the place, and these were new levies: neither did he think it advisable, upon his first landing, to expose the army to wounds and fatigue; more especially, as the town was strongly fortified, and extremely difficult of access, and a great body of horse was said to be upon the point of arrival to succor the inhabitants; he therefore thought it advisable not to remain and besiege the town, lest while he pursued that design, the enemy's cavalry should come behind and surround him.

6

But as he was drawing off his men, the garrison made a sudden sally; and the cavalry which had been sent by Juba to receive their pay, happening just then to come up, they took possession of the camp Caesar had left, and began to harass his rear. This being perceived, the legionaries immediately halted; and the cavalry, though few in number, boldly charged the vast multitude of the enemy. An incredible event occurred, that less than thirty Gallic horse repulsed two thousand Moors, and drove them into the town. Having thus repulsed the enemy and compelled them to retire behind their walls, Caesar resumed his intended march: but observing that they often repeated their sallies, renewing the pursuit from time to time, and again fleeing when attacked by the horse, he posted a few of the veteran cohorts which he had with him, with part of the cavalry, in the rear, and so proceeded slowly on his march. The further he advanced from the town, the less eager were the Numidians to pursue. Meantime, deputies arrived from the several towns and castles on the road, offering to furnish him with corn, and to perform whatever he might command. Toward the evening of that day, which was the calends of January, he fixed his camp at Ruspina.

7

Thence he removed and came before Leptis, a free city and governed by its own laws. Here he was met by deputies from the town, who, in the name of the inhabitants, offered their free submission. Whereupon, placing centurions and a guard before the gates, to prevent the soldiers from entering, or offering violence to any of the inhabitants, he himself encamped toward the shore, not far distant from the town. Hither by accident arrived some of the galleys and transports; by whom he was informed that the rest of the fleet, uncertain what course to pursue, had been steering for Utica. In the mean time Caesar could not depart from the sea, nor seek the inland provinces, on account of the error committed by the fleet. He likewise sent the cavalry back to their ships, probably to hinder the country from being plundered, and ordered fresh water to be carried to them on board. Meanwhile the Moorish horse rose suddenly, Caesar's party not expecting it, on the rowers who had been employed in carrying water, as they came out of the ships, and wounded many with their darts and killed some. For the manner of these barbarians is, to lie in ambush with their horses among the valleys, and suddenly launch upon an enemy; they seldom choosing to engage hand to hand in a plain.

8

In the mean time, Caesar dispatched letters and messengers into Sardinia and the neighboring provinces, with orders, as soon as they read the letters, to send supplies of men, corn, and warlike stores; and having unloaded part of the fleet, detached it, with Rabirius Posthumus, into Sicily, to bring over the second embarkation. At the same time he ordered out ten galleys, to get intelligence of the transports that had missed their way, and to maintain the freedom of the sea. He also ordered C. Sallustius Prispus, the praetor, at the head of a squadron, to sail to Percina, then in the hands of the enemy, because he heard there was great quantity of corn in that island: he gave these orders and instructions in such a manner as to leave no room for excuse or delay. Meanwhile, having informed himself, from the deserters and natives, of the condition of Scipio and his followers; and understanding that they were at the whole charge of maintaining Juba's cavalry; he could not but pity the infatuation of men, who thus chose to be tributaries to the king of Numidia, rather than securely enjoy their fortunes at home with their fellow-citizens.

9

Caesar moved his camp on the third day before the nones of January; and leaving six cohorts at Leptis, under the command of Saserna, returned with the rest of the forces to Ruspina, whence he had come the day before. Here he deposited the baggage of the army; and marching out with a light body of troops to forage, ordered the inhabitants to follow with their horses and carriages. Having by this means got together a great quantity of corn, he came back to Ruspina. I think that he acted with this intention, that by keeping possession of the maritime cities, and providing them with garrisons, he might secure a retreat for his fleet.

10

Leaving therefore P. Saserna, the brother of him who commanded at Leptis, to take charge of the town, with one legion, he orders all the wood that could be found to be carried into the place; and set out in person from Ruspina, with seven cohorts, part of the veteran legions who had behaved so well in the fleet under Sulpicius and Vatinius; and marching directly for the port, which lies at about two miles' distance, embarked with them in the evening, without imparting his intentions to the army, who were extremely inquisitive concerning the general's design. His departure occasioned the utmost sadness and consternation among the troops; for being few in number, mostly new levies, and those not all suffered to land, they saw themselves exposed, upon a foreign coast, to the mighty forces of a crafty nation, supported by an innumerable cavalry. Nor had they any resource in their present circumstances, or expectation of safety in their own conduct; but derived all their hope from the alacrity, vigor, and wonderful cheerfulness that appeared in their general's countenance; for he was of an intrepid spirit, and behaved with undaunted resolution and confidence. On his conduct, therefore, they entirely relied, and hoped to a man, that by his skill and talents, all difficulties would vanish before them.

11

Caesar, having continued the whole night on board, prepared to set sail about day-break; when, all on a sudden, the part of the fleet that had caused so much anxiety, appeared unexpectedly in view. Wherefore, ordering his men to quit their ships immediately, and receive the rest of the troops in arms upon the shore, he made the new fleet enter the port with the utmost diligence; and landing all the forces, horse and foot, returned again to Ruspina. Here he established his camp; and taking with him thirty cohorts, without baggage, advanced into the country to forage. Thus was Caesar's purpose at length discovered: that he meant, unknown to the enemy, to have sailed to the assistance of the transports that had missed their way, lest they should unexpectedly fall in with the African fleet. And he did not wish his own soldiers who were left behind in garrison to know this, lest they should be intimidated by the smallness of their numbers, and the multitude of the enemy.

12

Caesar had not marched above three miles from his camp, when he was informed by his scouts, and some advanced parties of horse, that the enemy's forces were in view. As soon as this announcement was made, a great cloud of dust began to appear. Upon this intelligence, Caesar ordered all his horse, of which he had at that time but a very small number, to advance, as likewise his archers, only a few of whom had followed him from the camp; and the legions to march quietly after him in order of battle; while he went forward at the head of a small party. Soon after, having discovered the enemy at some distance, he commanded the soldiers to repair to their arms, and prepare for battle. Their number in all did not exceed thirty cohorts, with four hundred horse, and one hundred and fifty archers.

13

Meanwhile the enemy, under the command of Labienus, and the two Pacidii, drew up, with a very large front, consisting not so much of foot as of horse, whom they intermixed with light-armed Numidians and archers; forming themselves in such close order, that Caesar's army, at a distance, mistook them all for infantry; and strengthening their right and left with many squadrons of horse. Caesar drew up his army in a single line, being obliged to do so by the smallness of his numbers; covering his front with his archers, and placing his cavalry on the right and left wings, with particular instructions not to suffer themselves to be surrounded by the enemy's numerous horse; for he imagined that he would have to fight only with infantry.

14

As both sides stood in expectation of the signal, and Caesar would not stir from his post, as he saw that with such few troops against so great a force he must depend more on stratagem than strength, on a sudden the enemy's horse began to extend themselves, and move in a lateral direction, so as to encompass the hills and weaken Caesar's horse, and at the same time to surround them. The latter could scarcely keep their ground against their numbers. Meanwhile, both the main bodies advancing to engage, the enemy's cavalry, intermixed with some light-armed Numidians, suddenly sprang forward, from their crowded troops, and attacked the legions with a shower of darts. Our men, preparing to return the charge, their horse retreated a little, while the foot continued to maintain their ground, till the others, having rallied, came on again, with fresh vigor, to sustain them.

15

Caesar perceived that his ranks were in danger of being broken by this new way of fighting, for our foot, in pursuing the enemy's horse, having advanced a considerable way beyond their colors, were wounded in the flank by the nearest Numidian darts, while the enemy's horse easily escaped our infantry's javelins by flight; he therefore gave express orders that no soldier should advance above four feet beyond the ensigns. Meanwhile, Labienus's cavalry, confiding in their numbers endeavored to surround those of Caesar: who being few in number, and overpowered by the multitude of the enemy, were forced to give ground a little, their horses being much wounded. The enemy pressed on more and more; so that in an instant, the legions, being surrounded on all sides by the enemy's cavalry, were obliged to form themselves into a circle, and fight, as if inclosed with barriers.

16

Labienus, with his head uncovered, advanced on horseback to the front of the battle, sometimes encouraging his own men, sometimes addressing Caesar's legions thus: "So ho! you raw soldiers there!" says he, "why so fierce? Has he infatuated you too with his words? Truly he has brought you into a fine condition! I pity you sincerely." Upon this, one of the soldiers said: "I am none of your raw warriors, Labienus, but a veteran of the tenth legion." " Where's your standard?" replied Labienus. " I'll soon make you sensible who I am," answered the soldier. Then pulling off his helmet, to discover himself, he threw a javelin, with all his strength at Labienus, which wounding his horse severely in the breast-"Know, Labienus," says he, "that this dart was thrown by a soldier of the tenth legion." However, the whole army was not a little daunted, especially the new levies; and began to cast their eyes upon Caesar, minding nothing, for the present, but to defend themselves from the enemy's darts.

17

Caesar meanwhile, perceiving the enemy's design, endeavored to extend his line of battle, as much as possible, directing the cohorts to face about alternately to the right and left. By this means, he broke the enemy's circle with his right and left wings; and attacking one part of them, thus separated from the other, with his horse and foot, at last put them to flight. He pursued them but a little way, fearing an ambuscade, and returned again to his own men. The same was done by the other division of Caesar's horse and foot, so that the enemy being driven back, and severely wounded on all sides, he retreated toward his camp, in order of battle.

18

Meantime M. Petreius, and Cn. Piso, with eleven hundred select Numidian horse, and a considerable body of foot, arrived to the assistance of the enemy; who, recovering from their terror, upon this reinforcement, and again resuming courage, fell upon the rear of the legions, as they retreated, and endeavored to hinder them from reaching their camp. Caesar, perceiving this, ordered his men to wheel about, and renew the battle in the middle of the plain. As the enemy still pursued their former plan, and avoided a closing engagement, and the horses of Caesar's cavalry had not yet recovered the fatigue of their late voyage, and were besides weakened with thirst, weariness, wounds, and of course unfit for a vigorous and long pursuit, which even the time of the day would not allow, he ordered both horse and foot to fall at once briskly upon the enemy, and not slacken the pursuit till they had driven them quite beyond the furthest hills, and taken possession of them themselves. Accordingly, upon a signal being given, when the enemy were throwing their javelins in a faint and careless manner, he suddenly charged them with his horse and foot; who in a moment driving them from the field, and over the adjoining hill, kept possession of that post for some time, and then retired slowly, in order of battle, to their camp. The enemy, who, in this last attack, had been very roughly handled, then at length retreated to their fortifications.

19

Meanwhile the action being over, a great number of deserters, of all kinds, flocked to Caesar's camp, besides multitudes of horse and foot that were made prisoners. From them we learned that it was the design of the enemy to have astonished our raw troops, with their new and uncommon manner of fighting; and after surrounding them with their cavalry, to have cut them to pieces, as they had done Curio; and that they had marched against us expressly with that intention. Labienus had even said, in the council of war, that he would lead such a numerous body of auxiliaries against his adversaries, as should fatigue us with the very slaughter, and defeat us even in the bosom of victory; for he relied more on the number than the valor of his troops. He had heard of the mutiny of the veteran legions at Rome, and their refusal to go into Africa; and was likewise well assured of the fidelity of his troops, who had served three years under him in Africa. He had a great number of Numidian cavalry and light-armed troops, besides the Gallic and German horse, whom he had drawn together out of the remains of Pompey's army, and carried over with him from Brundusium: he had likewise the freed men raised in the country, and trained to use bridled horses; and also the immense number of Juba's forces, his hundred and twenty elephants, his innumerable cavalry and legionaries, amounting to above twelve thousand. Emboldened by the hope such mighty forces raised in him, on the day before the nones of January, three days after Caesar's arrival, he came against him, with sixteen hundred Gallic and German horse, nine hundred under Petreius, eight thousand Numidians, four times that number of light-armed foot, with a multitude of archers and slingers. The battle lasted from the fifth hour till sunset, during which time Petreius, receiving a dangerous wound, was obliged to quit the field.

20

Meantime Caesar fortified his camp with much greater care, reinforced the guards, and threw up two intrenchments; one from Ruspina quite to the sea, the other from his camp to the sea likewise, to secure the communication, and receive supplies without danger. He landed a great number darts and military engines, armed part of the mariners, Gauls, Rhodians, and others, that after the example of the enemy he might have a number of light-armed troops to intermix with his cavalry. He likewise strengthened his army with a great number of Syrian and Iturean archers whom he drew from the fleet into his camp: for he understood that within three days Scipio was expected to unite his forces to Labienus and Petreius, and his army was said to consist of eight legions and three thousand horse. At the same time he established workshops, made a great number of darts and arrows, provided himself with leaden bullets and palisades, wrote to Sicily for hurdles and wood to make rams, because he had none in Africa, and likewise gave orders for sending corn; for the harvest in that country was like to be inconsiderable, the enemy having taken all the laborers into their service the year before, and stored up the grain in a few fortified towns, after demolishing the rest, forcing the inhabitants into the garrisoned places, and exhausting the whole country.

21

In this necessity, by paying court to private individuals, he obtained a small supply, and husbanded it with care. In the mean time he went round the works in person daily, and kept about four cohorts constantly on duty, on account of the multitude of the enemy. Labienus sent his sick and wounded, of which the number was very considerable, in wagons to Adrumetum. Meanwhile Caesar's transports, unacquainted with the coast, or where their general had landed wandered up and down in great uncertainty; and being, attacked, one after another, by the enemy's coasters, were, for the most part, either taken or burned. Caesar, being informed of this, stationed his fleet along the coast and islands for the security of his convoys.

22

Meanwhile M. Cato, who commanded in Utica, never ceased urging and exhorting young Pompey, in words to this effect: "Your father, when he was at your age, and observed the commonwealth oppressed by wicked and daring men, and the party of order either slain or driven into banishment from their country and relations, incited by the greatness of his mind and the love of glory, though then very young, and only a private man, had yet the courage to rally the remains of his father's army, and assert the freedom of Italy and Rome, which was almost crushed forever. He also recovered Sicily, Africa, Numidia, Mauritania, with amazing dispatch, and by that means gained an illustrious and extensive reputation among all nations, and triumphed while very young and only a Roman knight. Nor did he enter upon the administration of public affairs, distinguished by the shining exploits of his father, or the fame and reputation of his ancestors, or the honors and dignities of the state. Will you, on the contrary, possessed of these honors, and the reputation acquired by your father, sufficiently distinguished by your own industry and greatness of mind, not bestir yourself, join your father's friends, and give the earnestly required assistance to yourself, the republic, and every man of worth?"

23

The youth, roused by the remonstrances of that grave and worthy senator, got together about thirty sail, of all sorts, of which some few were ships of war, and sailing from Utica to Mauritania, invaded the kingdom of Bogud. And leaving his baggage behind him, with an army of two thousand men, partly freedmen, partly slaves, some armed, some not, approached the town of Ascurum, in which the king had a garrison. On the arrival of Pompey, the inhabitants suffered him to advance to the very walls and gates; when, suddenly sallying out, they drove back his troops in confusion and dismay to the sea and their ships. This ill-success determined him to leave that coast, nor did he afterward land in any place, but steered directly for the Balearean Isles.

24

Meantime Scipio, leaving a strong garrison at Utica, began his march, with the forces we have described above, and encamped first at

Adrumetum; and then, after a stay of a few days, setting out in the night, he joined Petreius and Labienus, lodging all the forces in one camp, about three miles distant from Caesar's. Their cavalry made continual excursions to our very works, and intercepted those who ventured too far in quest of wood or water, and obliged us to keep within our intrenchments. This soon occasioned a great scarcity of provision among Caesar's men, because no supplies had yet arrived from Sicily and Sardinia. The season, too, was dangerous for navigation, and he did not possess above six miles in each direction, in Africa, and was moreover greatly distressed for want of forage. The veteran soldiers and cavalry, who had been engaged in many wars both by sea and land, and often struggled with wants and misfortunes of this kind, gathering sea-weed, and washing it in fresh water, by that means subsisted their horses and cattle.

25

While things were in this situation, king Juba, being informed of Caesar's difficulties, and the few troops he had with him, resolved not to allow him time to remedy his wants or increase his forces. Accordingly he left his kingdom, at the head of a large body of horse and foot, and marched to join his allies. Meantime P. Sitius, and king Bogud, having intelligence of Juba's march, joined their forces, entered Numidia, and laying siege to Cirta, the most opulent city in the county, carried it in a few days, with two others belonging to the Getulians. They had offered the inhabitants leave to depart in safety, if they would peaceably deliver up the town; but these conditions being rejected, they were taken by storm, and the citizens all put to the sword. They continued to advance, and incessantly harassed the cities and country; of which Juba having intelligence, though he was upon the point of joining Scipio and the other chiefs, determined that it was better to march to the relief of his own kingdom, than run the hazard of being driven from it while he was assisting others, and, perhaps, after all, miscarry too in his designs against Caesar. He therefore retired, with his troops, leaving only thirty elephants behind him, and marched to the relief of his own cities and territories.

26

Meanwhile Caesar, as there was a doubt in the province concerning his arrival, and no one believed that he had come in person, but that some of his lieutenants had come over with the forces lately sent, dispatched letters to all the several states, to inform them of his presence. Upon this, many persons of rank fled to his camp, complaining of the barbarity and cruelty of the enemy. Caesar deeply touched by their tears and complaints, although before he had remained inactive, resolved to take the field as soon as the weather would permit, and he could draw his troops together. He immediately dispatched letters into Sicily, to Allienus and Rabirius Posthumus the praetors [to tell them] that without delay or excuse, either of the winter or the winds, they must send over the rest of the troops, to save Africa from utter ruin; because, without some speedy remedy, not a single house would be left standing, nor any thing escape the fury and ravages of the enemy. And he himself was so anxious and impatient, that from the day the letters were sent, he complained without ceasing of the delay of the fleet, and had his eyes night and day turned toward the sea. Nor was it wonderful; for he saw the villages burned, the country laid waste, the cattle destroyed, the towns plundered, the principal citizens either slain or put in chains, and their children dragged into servitude under the name of hostages; nor could he, amid all this scene of misery, afford any relief to those who implored his protection, on account of the small number of his forces. In the mean time he kept the soldiers incessantly at work upon the intrenchments, built forts and redoubts, and carried on his lines quite to the sea.

27

Meanwhile Scipio made use of the following contrivance for training and disciplining his elephants. He drew up two parties in order of battle; one of slingers, who were to act as enemies, and discharge small stones against the elephants: and fronting them, the elephants themselves, in one line, and his whole army behind him in battle-array; that when the enemy, by their discharge of stones, had frightened the elephants, and forced them to turn upon their own men, they might again be made to face the enemy, by the volleys of stones from the army behind them. The work however, went on but slowly, because these animals, after many years' training, are dangerous to both parties when brought into the field.

28

While the two generals were thus employed near Ruspina, C. Virgilius, a man of praetorian rank, who commanded in Thapsus, a maritime city, observing some of Caesar's transports that had missed their way, uncertain where Caesar had landed or held his camp; and thinking that a fair opportunity offered of destroying them, manned a galley that was in the port with soldiers and archers, and joining with it a few armed barks, began to pursue Caesar's ships. Though he was repulsed on several occasions he still pursued his design, and at last fell in with one, on board of which were two young Spaniards, of the name of Titius, who were tribunes of the fifth legion, and whose father had been made a senator by Caesar. There was with them a centurion of the same legion, T. Salienus by name, who had invested the house of M. Messala, Caesar's lieutenant, at Messana, and made use of very seditious language; nay, had even seized the money and ornaments destined for Caesar's triumph, and for that reason dreaded his resentment. He, conscious of his demerits, persuaded the young men to surrender themselves to Virgilius, by whom they were sent under a strong guard to Scipio, and three days after put to death. It is said, that the elder Titius begged of the centurions who were charged with the execution, that he might be first put to death; which being easily granted, they both suffered according to their sentence.

29

The cavalry that mounted guard in the two camps were continually skirmishing with one another. Sometimes too the German and Gallic cavalry of Labienus entered into discourse with those of Caesar, after promising not to injure one another. Meantime Labienus, with a party of horse, endeavored to surprise the town of Leptis, which Saserna guarded with three cohorts; but was easily repulsed, because the town was strongly fortified, and well provided with warlike engines; he however renewed the attempt several times. One day, as a strong squadron of the enemy had posted themselves before the gate, their officer being slain by an arrow discharged from a cross-bow, and pinned to his own shield, the rest were terrified and took to flight; by which means the town was delivered from any further attempts.

30

At the same time Scipio daily drew up his troops in order of battle, about three hundred paces from his camp; and after continuing in arms the greatest part of the day, retreated again to his camp in the evening. This he did several times, no one mean while offering to stir out of Caesar's camp, or approach his forces; which forbearance and tranquillity gave him such a contempt of Caesar and his army, that drawing out all his forces, and his thirty elephants, with towers on their backs, and extending his horse and foot as wide as possible, he approached quite up to Caesar's intrenchments.

31

Upon perceiving this, Caesar, quietly, and without noise or confusion, recalled to his camp all that were gone out either in quest of forage, wood, or to work upon the fortifications: he likewise ordered the cavalry that were upon guard not to quit their post until the enemy were within reach of dart; and if they then persisted in advancing, to retire in good order within the intrenchments. He ordered the rest of the cavalry to be ready and armed, each in his own place. These orders were not given by himself in person, or after viewing the disposition of the enemy from the rampart; but such was his consummate knowledge of the art of war, that he gave all the necessary directions by his officers, he himself sitting in his tent, and informing himself of the motions of the enemy by his scouts. He very well knew, that, whatever confidence the enemy might have in their numbers, they would yet never dare to attack the camp of a general who had so often repulsed, terrified, and put them to flight; who had frequently pardoned and granted them their lives; and whose very name had weight and authority enough to intimidate their army. He was besides well intrenched with a high rampart and deep ditch, the approaches to which were rendered so difficult by the sharp spikes which he had disposed in a very skillful manner, that they were even sufficient of themselves to keep off the enemy. He had also a large supply of cross-bows, engines, and all sorts of weapons necessary for a vigorous defense, which he had prepared on account of the fewness of his troops, and the inexperience of his new levies. It was not owing to being influenced by the fear of the enemy or their numerical strength, that he allowed himself to appear daunted in their estimation. And it was not owing to his having any doubts of gaining the victory that he did not lead his troops to action, although they were raw and few, but he thought that it was a matter of great importance, what sort the victory should be: for he thought that it would disgrace him, if after so many noble exploits, and defeating such powerful armies, and after gaining so many glorious victories, he should appear to have gained a bloody victory over the remnants who had rallied after their flight. He determined, in consequence of this, to endure the pride and exultation of his enemies, until some portion of his veteran legion should arrive in the second embarkation.

32

Scipio, after a short stay before the intrenchments, as if in contempt of Caesar, withdrew slowly to his camp: and having called the soldiers together, enlarged upon the terror and despair of the enemy, when encouraging his men, he assured them of a complete victory in a short time. Caesar made his soldiers again return to the works, and under pretense of fortifying his camp, inured the new levies to labor and fatigue. Meantime the Numidians and Getulians deserted daily from Scipio's camp. Part returned home; part came over to Caesar, because they understood he was related to C. Marius, from whom their ancestors had received considerable favors. Of these he selected some of distinguished rank, and sent them home, with letters to their countrymen, exhorting them to levy troops for their own defense, and not to listen to the suggestions of his enemies.

33

While these things were passing near Ruspina, deputies from Acilla, a free town, and all the neighboring towns, arrived in Caesar's camp, and promised "to be ready to execute Caesar's commands, and to do so withal, and that they only begged and requested of him to give them garrisons, that they might do so in safety and without danger to themselves, that they would furnish them with corn and whatever supplies they had, to secure the common safety. Caesar readily complied with their demands, and having assigned a garrison, sent C.

Messius, who had been aedile, to command in Acilla. Upon intelligence of this, Considius Longus, who was at Adrumetum with two legions and seven hundred horse, leaving a garrison in that city, hastened to Acilla at the head of eight cohorts: but Messius, having accomplished his march with great expedition, arrived there before him. When Considius, therefore, approached, and found Caesar's garrison in possession of the town, not daring to make any attempt, he returned again to Adrumetum. But some days after, Labienus having sent him a reinforcement of horse, he began to besiege the town.

34

Much about the same time, C. Sallustius Crispus, who, as we have seen, had been sent a few days before to Cercina with a fleet, arrived in that island. Upon his arrival, C. Decimus the quaestor, who, with a strong party of his own domestics, had charge of the magazines erected there, went on board a small vessel and fled. Sallustius meanwhile was well received by the Cercinates, and finding great store of corn in the island, loaded all the ships then in the port, whose number was very considerable, and dispatched them to Caesar's camp. At the same time Allienus, the proconsul, put on board of the transports at Lilybaeum the thirteenth and fourteenth legions, with eight hundred Gallic horse and a thousand archers and slingers, and sent the second embarkation to Africa, to Caesar. This fleet meeting with a favorable wind, arrived in four days at Ruspina, where Caesar had his camp. Thus he experienced a double pleasure on this occasion, receiving at one and the same time, both a supply of provisions and a reinforcement of troops, which animated the soldiers, and delivered them from the apprehensions of want. Having landed the legions and cavalry, he allowed them some time to recover from the fatigue and sickness of their voyage, and then distributed them into the forts, and along the works.

35

Scipio and the other generals were greatly surprised at this conduct, and could not conceive why Caesar, who had always been forward and active in war, should all of a sudden change his measures; which they therefore suspected must proceed from some very powerful reasons. Uneasy and disturbed to see him so patient, they made choice of two

Getulians, on whose fidelity they thought they could rely; and promising them great rewards, sent them, under the name of deserters, to get intelligence of Caesar's designs. When they were brought before him, they begged they might have leave to speak without personal danger, which being granted, "It is now a long time, great general," said they, "since many of us Getulians, clients of C. Marius, and almost all Roman citizens of the fourth and sixth legions, have wished for an opportunity to come over to you; but have hitherto been prevented by the guards of Numidian horse, from doing it without great risk. Now we gladly embrace the occasion, being sent by Scipio under the name of deserters, to discover what ditches and traps you have prepared for his elephants, how you intended to oppose these animals, and what dispositions you are making for battle." They were praised by Caesar, and liberally rewarded, and sent to the other deserters. We had soon a proof of the truth of what they had advanced; for the next day a great many soldiers of these legions, mentioned by the Getulians, deserted to Caesar's camp.

36

While affairs were in this posture at Ruspina, M. Cato, who commanded in Utica, was daily enlisting freed-men, Africans, slaves, and all that were of age to bear arms, and sending them without intermission to Scipio's camp. Meanwhile deputies from the town of Tisdra came to Caesar to inform him, that some Italian merchants had brought three hundred thousand bushels of corn into that city, and to demand a garrison as well for their own defense as to secure the corn. Caesar thanked the deputies, promised to send the garrison they desired, and having encouraged them, sent them back to their fellow-citizens. Meantime P. Sitius entered Numidia with his troops, and took by storm a castle situated on a mountain, where Juba had laid up a great quantity of provisions, and other things necessary for carrying on the war.

37

Caesar, having increased his forces with two veteran legions, and all the cavalry and light-armed troops that had arrived in the second embarkation, detached six transports to Lilybaeum, to bring over the rest of the army. He himself on the sixth day before the calends of

February, ordering the scouts and lictors to attend him at six in the evening, drew out all the legions at midnight, and directed his march toward Ruspina, where he had a garrison, and which had first declared in his favor, no one knowing or having the least suspicion of his design. Thence he continued his route, by the left of the camp, along the sea, and passed a little declivity, which opened into a fine plain, extending fifteen miles, and bordering upon a chain of mountains of moderate height, that formed a kind of theater. In this ridge were some hills that rose higher than the rest, on which forts and watchtowers had formerly been erected, and at the furthest of which, Scipio's guards and out-posts were stationed.

38

After Caesar gained the ridge, which I have just mentioned, and began to raise redoubts upon the several eminences (which he executed in less than half an hour), and when he was not very far from the last, which bordered on the enemy's camp, and where, as we have said, Scipio had his out-guard of Numidians, he stopped a moment; and having taken a view of the ground, and posted his cavalry in the most commodious situation, he ordered the legions to throw up an intrenchment along the middle of the ridge, from the place at which he was arrived to that whence he set out. When Scipio and Labienus observed this, they drew all their cavalry out of the camp, formed them in order of battle, and advancing about a mile, posted their infantry by way of a second line, somewhat less than half a mile from their camp.

39

Caesar was unmoved by the appearance of the enemy's forces, and encouraged his men to go on with the work. But when he perceived that they were within fifteen hundred paces of the intrenchment, and saw that the enemy were coming nearer to interrupt and disturb the soldiers and oblige him to draw off the legions from the work, he ordered a squadron of Spanish cavalry, supported by some light-armed infantry, to attack the Numidian guard upon the nearest eminence, and drive them from that post. They accordingly, advancing rapidly, attacked the Numidian cavalry: they took some of them alive, severely wounded several in their flight, and made themselves masters of the place. This being observed by Labienus, he wheeled off almost the whole right wing of the horse, that he might the more effectually succor the fugitives. Caesar waited till he was at a considerable distance from his own men, and then detached his left wing to intercept the enemy.

40

In the plain where this happened was a large villa, with four turrets, which prevented Labienus from seeing that he was intercepted by Caesar's cavalry. He had therefore no apprehension of the approach of Caesar's horse till he found himself charged in the rear; which struck such a sudden terror into the Numidian cavalry that they immediately betook themselves to flight. The Gauls and Germans who stood their ground, being surrounded on all sides, were entirely cut off. This being perceived by Scipio's legions, who were drawn up in order of battle before the camp, they fled in the utmost terror and confusion. Scipio and his forces being driven from the plain and the hills, Caesar sounded a retreat, and ordered all the cavalry to retire behind the works. When the field was cleared, he could not forbear admiring the huge bodies of the Gauls and Germans, who had been partly induced by the authority of Labienus to follow him out of Gaul, and partly drawn over by promises and rewards. Some being made prisoners in the battle with Curio, and having their lives granted them, continued faithful out of gratitude. Their bodies, of surprising symmetry and size, lay scattered all over the plain.

41

Next day, Caesar drew all his forces together, and formed them in order of battle upon the plain. Scipio, discouraged by so unexpected a check, and the number of his wounded and slain, kept within his lines. Caesar, with his army in battle array, marched along the roots of the hills, and gradually approached his trenches. Caesar's legions were, by this time, not more than a mile from Uzita, a town possessed by Scipio, when the latter, fearing lest he should lose the town, whence he procured water and other conveniences for his army, resolved therefore to preserve it, at all hazards, and brought forth his whole army, and drew them up in four lines, forming the first of cavalry, supported by elephants with castles on their backs. Caesar believing that Scipio approached with the intention of giving battle, continued where he was posted, not far from the town. Scipio meanwhile, having the town in the center of his front, extended his two wings, where were his elephants, in full view of our army.

42

When Caesar had waited till sunset, without finding that Scipio stirred from his post, who seemed rather disposed to defend himself by his advantageous situation, than hazard a battle in the open field, he did not think proper to advance further that day, because the enemy had a strong garrison of Numidians in the town, which besides covered the center of their front: and he foresaw great difficulty in forming, at the same time, an attack upon the town, and opposing their right and left, with the advantage of the ground; especially as the soldiers had continued under arms and fasted since morning. Having therefore led back his troops to their camp, he resolved next day to extend his lines nearer the town.

43

Meantime Considius, who was besieging eight mercenary cohorts of Numidians and Getulians in Acilla, where P. Messius commanded, after continuing long before the place, and seeing all his works burned and destroyed by the enemy, upon the report of the late battle of the cavalry, set fire to is corn, destroyed his wine, oil, and other stores, which were necessary for the maintenance of his army; and abandoning the siege of Acilla, divided his forces with Scipio, and retired through the kingdom of Juba, to Adrumetum.

44

Meanwhile one of the transports, belonging to the second embarkation, which Allienus had sent from Sicily, in which were Q. Cominius, and L. Ticida, a Roman knight, being separated from the rest of the fleet, in a storm, and driven to Thapsus, was taken by Virgilius, and all the persons on board sent to Scipio. A three-banked galley likewise, belonging to the same fleet, being forced by the winds to Aegimurum, was intercepted by the squadron under Varus and M. Octavius. In this vessel were some veteran soldiers, with a centurion, and a few new levies, whom Varus treated without insult, and sent under a guard to Scipio. When they came into his presence, and appeared before his tribunal: "I am satisfied," said he, "it is not by your own inclination, but at the instigation of your wicked general, that you impiously wage war on your fellow-citizens, and every man of worth. If, therefore, now that fortune has put you in our power, you will take this opportunity to unite with the good citizens, in the defense of the commonwealth, I am determined to give you life and money: therefore speak openly your sentiments."

45

Scipio having ended his speech, and expecting a thankful return to so gracious an offer, permitted them to reply; one of their number, a centurion of the fourteenth legion, thus addressed him: "Scipio," says he ("for I can not give you the appellation of general), I return you my hearty thanks for the good treatment you are willing to show to prisoners of war; and perhaps I might accept of your kindness were it not to be purchased at the expense of a horrible crime. What! shall I carry arms, and fight against Caesar, my general, under whom I have served as centurion; and against his victorious army, to whose renown I have for more than thirty-six years endeavored to contribute by my valor? It is what I will never do, and even advise you not to push the war any further. You know not what troops you have to deal with, nor the difference betwixt them and yours: of which, if you please, I will give you an indisputable instance. Do you pick out the best cohort you have in your army, and give me only ten of my comrades, who are now your prisoners, to engage them: you shall see by the success, what you are to expect from your soldiers."

46

When the centurion had courageously made this reply, Scipio, incensed at his boldness, and resenting the affront, made a sign to some of his officers to kill him on the spot, which was immediately put in execution. At the same time, ordering the other veteran soldiers to be separated from the new levies, "Carry away." said he, "these men, contaminated by the pollution of crime, and pampered with the blood of their fellow-citizens." Accordingly they were conducted without the rampart, and cruelly massacred. The new-raised soldiers were distributed among his legions, and Cominius and Ticida forbade to appear in his presence. Caesar, concerned for his misfortune, broke, with ignominy, the officers whose instructions were to secure the coast, and advance to a certain distance into the main sea, to protect and facilitate the approach of the transports, but who had neglected their duty on that important station.

47

About this time a most incredible accident befell Caesar's army; for the Pleiades being set, about the second watch of the night, a terrible storm arose, attended by hail of an uncommon size. But what contributed to render this misfortune the greater was, that Caesar had not, like other generals, put his troops into winter quarters, but was every three or four days changing his camp, to gain ground on the enemy; which keeping the soldiers continually employed they were utterly unprovided with any conveniences to protect them from the inclemency of the weather. Besides, he had brought over his army from Sicily with such strictness, that neither officer nor soldier had been permitted to take their equipages or utensils with them, nor so much as a vessel or a single slave; and so far had they been from acquiring or providing themselves with any thing in Africa, that, on account of the great scarcity of provisions, they had even consumed their former stores. Impoverished by these accidents, very few of them had tents; the rest had made themselves a kind of covering, either by spreading their clothes, or with mats and rushes. But these being soon penetrated by the storm and hail, the soldiers had no resource left, but wandered up and down the camp, covering their heads with their bucklers to shelter them from the violence of the weather. In a short time the whole camp was under water, the fires extinguished, and all their provisions washed away or spoiled. The same night the shafts of the javelins belonging to the fifth legion, of their own accord, took fire.

48

In the mean time, king Juba, having been informed of the cavalry actions with Scipio, and being earnestly solicited, by letters from that general, to come to his assistance, left Sabura at home with part of the army, to carry on the war against Sitius, and that he might add the weight of his authority to free Scipio's troops from the dread they had of Caesar, began his march, with three legions, eight hundred regular horse, a body of Numidian cavalry, great numbers of light-armed infantry, and thirty elephants. When he arrived he lodged himself, with those forces which I have described, in a separate camp, at no great distance from that of Scipio. (Great alarm had prevailed for some time previously in Caesar's camp, and the report of his approach had increased and produced a general suspense and expectation among the troops. But his arrival, and the appearance of his camp, soon dispelled all these apprehensions; and they despised the king of Mauritania, now that he was present, as much as they had feared him when at a distance.) After this junction, any one might easily perceive that Scipio's courage and confidence were increased by the arrival of the king. For next day, drawing out all his own and the royal forces, with sixty elephants, he ranged them, in order of battle, with great ostentation advancing a little beyond his intrenchments, and, after a short stay, retreated to his camp.

49

Caesar, knowing that Scipio had received all the supplies he expected, and judging he would no longer decline coming to an engagement, began to advance along the ridge with his forces, extend his lines, secure them with redoubts, and possess himself of the eminences between him and Scipio. The enemy, confiding in their numbers, seized a neighboring hill, and thereby prevented the progress of our works. Labienus had formed the design of securing this post, and as it lay nearest his quarters, soon got thither.

50

There was a broad and deep valley, of rugged descent, broken with caves, which Caesar had to pass before he could come to the hill which he wished to occupy, and beyond which was a thick grove of old olives. Labienus, perceiving that Caesar must march this way, and having a perfect knowledge of the country, placed himself in ambush, with the light-armed foot and part of the cavalry. At the same time he disposed some horse behind the hills, that when he should fall unexpectedly upon Caesar's foot, they might suddenly advance from behind the mountain. And thus Caesar and his army being attacked in front and rear, surrounded with danger on all sides, and unable either to retreat or advance, would, he imagined, fall an easy prey to his victorious troops. Caesar, who had no suspicion of the ambuscade, sent his cavalry before; and arriving at the place, Labienus's men, either forgetting or neglecting the orders of their general, or fearing to be trampled to death in the ditch by our cavalry, began to issue in small parties from the rock, and ascend the hill. Caesar's horse pursuing them, slew some, and took others prisoners; then making toward the hill drove thence Labienus's detachment and immediately took possession. Labienus, with a small party of horse, escaped with great difficulty by flight.

51

The cavalry having thus cleared the mountain, Caesar resolved to intrench himself there, and distributed the work to the legions. He then ordered two lines of communication to be drawn from the greater camp, across the plain on the side of Uzita, which stood between him and the enemy, and was garrisoned by a detachment of Scipio's army, and place them in such a manner as to meet at the right and left angles of the town. His design in this work was, that when he approached the town with his troops, and began to attack it, these lines might secure his flanks, and hinder the enemy's horse from surrounding him, and compelling him to abandon the siege. It likewise gave his men more frequent opportunities of conversing with the enemy, and facilitated the means of desertion to such as favored his cause; many of whom had already come over, though not without great danger to themselves. He wanted also, by drawing nearer the enemy, to see if they really intended to come to an action, and in addition to all these reasons, that the place itself being very low, he might there sink some wells; whereas before he had a long and troublesome way to send for water. While the legions were employed in these works, part of the army stood ready drawn up before the trenches, and had frequent skirmishes with the Numidian horse and light-armed foot

52

A little before evening, when Caesar was drawing off his legions from the works, Juba, Scipio, and Labienus, at the head of all their horse and light-armed foot, fell furiously upon his cavalry; who, being overwhelmed by the sudden and general attack of so great a multitude, were forced to give ground a little. But the event was very different from what the enemy expected; for Caesar, leading back his legions to the assistance of his cavalry, they immediately rallied, turned upon the Numidians, and charging them vigorously while they were dispersed and disordered with the pursuit, drove them with great loss to the king's camp, and slew several of them. And had not night intervened, and the dust raised by the wind obstructed the prospect, Juba and Labienus would both have fallen into Caesar's hands, and their whole cavalry and light-armed infantry have been cut off. Meanwhile Scipio's men, of the fourth and sixth legions, left him in crowds, some deserting to Caesar's camp, others fleeing to such places as were most convenient for them. Curio's horse likewise, distrusting Scipio and his troops, followed the same counsel.

53

While these things were being carried on by Caesar and his opponents around Uzita, two legions, the ninth and tenth, sailing in transports from Sicily, when they came before Ruspina, observing Caesar's ships that lay at anchor about Thapsus, and fearing it might be the enemy's fleet stationed there to intercept them, imprudently stood out to sea; and after being long tossed by the winds, and harassed by thirst and famine, at last arrived at Caesar's camp.

54

Soon after these legions were landed, Caesar, calling to mind their former licentious behaviour in Italy, and the rapines of some of their officers, seized the slight pretext furnished by C. Avienus, a military tribune of the tenth legion, who, when he set out for Sicily, filled a ship entirely with his own slaves and horses, without taking on board one single soldier. Wherefore, summoning all the military tribunes and centurions to appear before his tribunal next day, he addressed them in these terms, "I could have wished that those, whose insolence and former licentious character have given me cause of complaint, had been capable of amendment, and of making a good use of my mildness, patience, and moderation. But since they know not how to confine themselves within due bounds, I intend to make an example of them, according to the law of arms, in order that others may be taught a better conduct. Because you, C. Avienus, when you were in Italy, instigated the soldiers of the Roman people to revolt from the republic and have been guilty of rapines and plunders in the municipal towns;

and because you have never been of any real service, either to the commonwealth or to your general, and in lieu of soldiers, have crowded the transports with your slaves and equipage; so that, through your fault, the republic is in want of soldiers, who at this time are not only useful, but necessary; for all these causes, I break you with ignominy, and order you to leave Africa this very day. In like manner I break you, A. Fonteius, because you have behaved yourself as a seditious officer, and as a bad citizen. You, T. Salienus, M. Tiro, C. Clusinus, have attained the rank of centurions through my indulgence, and not through your own merit; and since you have been invested with that rank, have neither shown bravery in war, nor good conduct in peace, and have been more zealous in raising seditions, and exciting the soldiers against your general than in observing forbearance and moderation. I therefore think you unworthy of continuing centurions in my army: I break you, and order you to quit Africa as soon as possible." Having concluded this speech, he delivered them over to some centurions, with orders to confine them separately on board a ship, allowing each of them a single slave to wait on him.

55

Meantime the Getulian deserters, whom Caesar had sent home with letters and instructions, as we related above, arrived among their countrymen: who, partly swayed by their authority, partly by the name and reputation of Caesar, revolted from Juba; and speedily and unanimously taking up arms, scrupled not to act in opposition to their king. Juba, having thus three wars to sustain, was compelled to detach six cohorts from the army destined to act against Caesar, and send them to defend the frontiers of his kingdom against the Getulians.

56

Caesar, having finished his lines of communication, and pushed them so near the town, as to be just out of reach of dart, intrenched himself there. He caused warlike engines in great numbers to be placed in the front of his works, wherewith he played perpetually against the town; and to increase the enemy's apprehensions, drew five legions out of his other camp. When this opportunity was presented, several persons of eminence and distinction earnestly requested an interview with their friends, and held frequent conferences, which Caesar foresaw would turn to his advantage. For the chief officers of the Getulian horse, with other illustrious men of that nation (whose fathers had served under C. Marius, and from his bounty obtained considerable estates in their country, but after Sylla's victory had been made tributaries to king Hiempsal), taking advantage of the night, when the fires were lighted, came over to Caesar's camp near Uzita, with their horses and servants, to the number of about a thousand.

57

When Scipio and his party learned this, and were much annoyed at the disaster, they perceived, much about the same time, M. Aquinius in discourse with C. Saserna. Scipio sent him word that he did not do well to correspond with the enemy. Aquinius, however, paid no attention to this reprimand, but pursued his discourse. Soon after, one of Juba's guards came to him and told him, in the hearing of Saserna, "The king forbids you to continue this conversation." He, being terrified by this order, immediately retired, and obeyed the command of the king. One can not wonder enough at this step in a Roman citizen, who had already attained to considerable honors in the commonwealth; that though neither banished his country, nor stripped of his possessions, he should pay a more ready obedience to the orders of a foreign prince than those of Scipio; and choose rather to behold the destruction of his party than return into the bosom of his country. And still greater insolence was shown by Juba, not to M. Aquinius, a man of no family, and an inconsiderable senator, but even to Scipio himself, a man of illustrious birth, distinguished honors, and high dignity in the state. For as Scipio, before the king's arrival, always wore a purple coat of mail, Juba is reported to have told him, that he ought not to wear the same habit as he did. Accordingly, Scipio changed his purple robe for a white one, submitting to Juba, a most haughty and insolent monarch.

58

Next day they drew out all their forces from both camps; and forming them on an eminence not far from Caesar's camp, continued thus in order of battle. Caesar likewise drew out his men, and disposed them in battle array before his lines; not doubting but the enemy, who exceeded him in number of troops, and had been so considerably reinforced by the arrival of king Juba, would advance to attack him. Wherefore, having ridden through the ranks, encouraged his men, and gave them the signal of battle, he stayed, expecting the enemy's charge. For he did not think it advisable to remove far from his lines: because the enemy having a strong garrison in Uzita, which was opposite to his right wing, he could not advance beyond that place without exposing his flank to a sally from the town. He was also deterred by the following reason, because the ground before Scipio's army was very rough, and he thought it likely to disorder his men in the charge.

59

And I think that I ought not to omit to describe the order of battle of both armies. Scipio drew up his troops in the following manner: he posted his own legions and those of Juba in the front; behind them the Numidians, as a body of reserve: but in so very thin ranks, and so far extended in length, that to see them at a distance you would have taken the main body for a simple line of legionaries, which was doubled only upon the wings. He placed elephants at equal distances on the right and left, and supported them by the light-armed troops and auxiliary Numidians. All the regular cavalry were on the right; for the left was covered by the town of Uzita, nor had the cavalry room to extend themselves on that side. Accordingly, he stationed the Numidian horse, with an incredible multitude of light-armed foot, about a thousand paces from his right, toward the foot of a mountain, considerably removed from his own and the enemy's troops. He did so with this intention, that, when the two armies should engage, his cavalry at the commencement of the action should take a longer sweep, inclose Caesar's army and throw them into confusion by their darts. Such was Scipio's disposition.

60

Caesar's order of battle, to describe it from left to right, was arranged in the following manner: the ninth and eighth legions formed the left wing: the thirteenth, fourteenth, twenty-eighth, and twenty-sixth, the main body; and the thirtieth and twenty-eighth the right. His second line on the right consisted partly of the cohorts of those legions we have already mentioned, partly of the new levies. His third line was posted to the left, extending as far as the middle legion of the main body, and so disposed, that the left wing formed a triple order of battle.

The reason of this disposition was, because his right wing being defended by the works, it behooved him to make his left stronger, that they might be a match for the numerous cavalry of the enemy; for which reason he had placed all his horse there, intermixed with light-armed foot; and as he could not rely much upon them, had detached the fifth legion to sustain them. He placed archers up and down the field, but principally in the two wings.

61

The two armies thus facing one another in order of battle, with a space of no more than three hundred paces between, continued so posted from morning till night without fighting, of which perhaps there was never an instance before. But when Caesar began to retreat within his lines, suddenly all the Numidian and Getulian horse without bridles, who were posted behind the enemy's army, made a motion to the right, and began to approach Caesar's camp on the mountain; while the regular cavalry under Labienus continued in their post to keep our legions in check. Upon this, part of Caesar's cavalry, with the light-armed foot, advancing hastily, and without orders, against the Getulians, and venturing to pass the morass, found themselves unable to deal with the superior multitude of the enemy; and being abandoned by the light-armed troops, were forced to retreat in great disorder, after the loss of one trooper, twenty-six light-armed foot, and many of their horses wounded. Scipio, overjoyed at this success, returned toward night to his camp. But fortune determined not to give such unalloyed joy to those engaged in war, for the day after, a party of horse, sent by Caesar to Leptis in quest of provisions, falling in unexpectedly with some Numidian and Getulian stragglers, killed or made prisoners about a hundred of them. Caesar, meanwhile, omitted not every day to draw out his men and labor at the works; carrying a ditch and rampart quite across the plain, to prevent the incursions of the enemy. Scipio likewise drew lines opposite to Caesar's, and used great exertions lest Caesar should cut off his communication with the mountain. Thus both generals were busied about their intrenchments, yet a day seldom passed, without some skirmish between the cavalry.

62

In the mean time, Varus, upon notice that the seventh and eighth legions had sailed from Sicily, speedily equipped the fleet he had brought to winter at Utica; and manning it with Getulian rowers and mariners, went out a cruising and came before Adrumetum with fifty-five ships. Caesar, ignorant of his arrival, sent L. Cispius, with a squadron of twenty-seven sail toward Thapsus, to anchor there for the security of his convoys; and likewise dispatched Q. Aquila to Adrumetum, with thirteen galleys, upon the same errand. Cispius soon reached the station appointed to him: but Aquila being attacked by a storm could not double the cape, which obliged him to put into a creek at some distance, that afforded convenient shelter. The rest of the fleet which remained at sea before Leptis, where the mariners having landed and wandered here and there upon the shore, some having gone into the town for the purpose of purchasing provisions, was left quite defenseless. Varus, having notice of this from a deserter, and resolving to take advantage of the enemy's negligence, left Adrumetum in Cothon at the commencement of the second watch, and arriving early next morning with his whole fleet before Leptis, burned all the transports that were out at sea, and took without opposition two five-benched galleys, in which were none to defend them.

63

Caesar had an account brought him of this unlucky accident, as he was inspecting the works of his camp. Whereupon he immediately took horse, and leaving every thing else, went full speed to Leptis, which was but two leagues distant, and going on board a brigantine, ordered all the ships to follow him. He soon came up with Aquila, whom he found dismayed and terrified at the number of ships he had to oppose; and continuing his course, began to pursue the enemy's fleet. Meantime Varus, astonished at Caesar's boldness and dispatch, tacked about with his whole fleet, and made the best of his way for Adrumetum. But Caesar, after four miles' sail, recovered one of his galleys, with the crew and a hundred and thirty of the enemy's men left to guard her; and took a three benched galley belonging to the enemy which had fallen astern during the engagement, with all the soldiers and mariners on board. The rest of the fleet doubled the cape, and made the port of Adrumetum in Cothon. Caesar could not double the cape with the same wind, but keeping the sea at anchor all night, appeared early next morning before Adrumetum. He set fire to all the transports without Cothon, and took what galleys he found there, or forced them into the harbor; and having waited some time to offer the enemy battle, returned again to his camp.

64

On board the ship he had taken was P. Vestrius, a Roman knight, and P. Ligarius, who had served in Spain under Afranius, the same who had prosecuted the war against him in Spain, and who, instead of acknowledging the conqueror's generosity, in granting him his liberty, had joined Pompey in Greece; and after the battle of Pharsalia, had gone into Africa, to Varus, there to continue in the service of the same cause. Caesar, to punish his perfidy and breach of oath, gave immediate orders for his execution. But he pardoned P. Vestrius, because his brother had paid his ransom at Rome, and because he himself proved, that being taken in Nasidius's fleet, and condemned to die, he had been saved by the kindness of Varus, since which no opportunity had offered of making his escape.

65

It is the custom of the people of Africa to deposit their corn privately in vaults, under ground, to secure it in time of war, and guard it from the sudden incursions of an enemy. Caesar, having intelligence of this from a spy, drew out two legions, with a party of cavalry, at midnight, and sent them about ten miles off; whence they returned, loaded with corn to the camp. Labienus, being informed of it, marched about seven miles, through the mountains Caesar had passed the day before, and there encamped with two legions; where expecting that Caesar would often come the same way in quest of corn, he daily lay in ambush with a great body of horse and light-armed foot.

66

Caesar, being informed of the ambuscade of Labienus by deserters, delayed there a few days, till the enemy, by repeating the practice often, had abated a little of their circumspection. Then suddenly, one morning ordering eight veteran legions with part of the cavalry to follow him by the Decuman gate, he sent forward the rest of the cavalry; who, coming suddenly upon the enemy's light-armed foot, that lay in ambush among the valleys, slew about five hundred, and put the rest to flight. Meantime Labienus advanced, with all his cavalry, to support the fugitives, and was on the point of overpowering our small party with his numbers, when suddenly Caesar appeared with the legions, in order of battle. This sight checked the ardor of Labienus, who thought proper to sound a retreat. The day after, Juba ordered all the Numidians who had deserted their post and fled to their camp to be crucified.

67

Meanwhile Caesar, being distressed by want of corn, recalled all his forces to the camp; and having left garrisons at Leptis, Ruspina, and Acilla, ordered Cispius and Aquila to blockade with their fleets, the one Adrumetum, the other Thapsus, and setting fire to his camp at Uzita, he set out, in order of battle, at the fourth watch, disposed his baggage on the left, and came to Agar, which had been often vigorously attacked by the Getulians, and as valiantly defended by the inhabitants. There encamping in the plain before the town, he went with part of his army round the country in quest of provisions; and having found a large store of barley, oil, wine, and figs, with a small quantity of wheat, after allowing the troops some time to refresh themselves, he returned to his camp. Scipio meanwhile hearing of Caesar's departure, followed him along the hills, with all his forces, and posted himself about six miles off; in three different camps.

68

The town of Zeta, lying on Scipio's side of the country, was not above ten miles from his camp, but might be about eighteen from that of Caesar. Scipio had sent two legions thither to forage; which Caesar having intelligence of from a deserter, removed his camp from the plain to a hill, for the greater security; and leaving a garrison there, marched at three in the morning with the rest of his forces, passed the enemy's camp, and possessed himself of the town. He found that Scipio's legions were gone further into the country to forage: against whom, setting out immediately, he found that the whole army had come up to their assistance, which obliged him to give over the pursuit. He took, on this occasion, C. Mutius Reginus, a Roman knight, Scipio's intimate friend, and governor of the town; also P. Atrius, a Roman knight, of the province of Utica, with twenty-two camels, belonging to king Juba. Then leaving a garrison in the place, under the command of Oppius, his lieutenant, he returned to his own camp.

69

As he drew near Scipio's camp, by which he was obliged to pass, Labienus and Afranius, who lay in ambuscade among the nearest hills, with all their cavalry and light-armed infantry, started up and attacked his rear. When Caesar perceived this, he detached his cavalry to receive their charge, ordered the legions to throw all their baggage into a heap, and face about upon the enemy. No sooner was this order executed than, upon the first charge of the legions, the enemy's horse and light-armed foot began to give way, and were with incredible ease driven from the higher ground. But when Caesar, supposing them sufficiently deterred from any further attempts, began to pursue his march, they again issued from the hills; and the Numidians, with the light armed infantry, who are wonderfully nimble, and accustom themselves to fight intermixed with the horse, with whom they keep an equal pace, either in advancing or retiring, fell a second time upon our foot. As they repeated this often, pressing upon our troops when we marched, and retiring when we endeavored to engage, always keeping at a certain distance, and with singular care avoiding a close fight, and considering it enough to wound us with their darts, Caesar plainly saw that their whole aim was to oblige him to encamp in that place, where no water was to be had; that his soldiers, who had tasted nothing from three in the morning till four in the afternoon, might perish with hunger, and the cattle with thirst.

70

When sunset now approached, and Caesar found he had not gained a hundred paces in four hours, and that by keeping his cavalry in the rear he lost many horse, he ordered the legions to fall behind, and close the march. Proceeding thus with a slow and gentle pace, he found the legions fitter to sustain the enemy's charge. Meantime the Numidian horse, wheeling round the hills, to the right and left, threatened to inclose Caesar's forces with their numbers, while part continued to harass his rear: and if but three or four veteran soldiers faced about, and darted their javelins at the enemy, no less than two thousand of them would tale to flight: but suddenly rallying, returned to the fight, and charged the legionaries with their darts. Thus Caesar, at one time marching forward, at another halting, and going on but slowly, reached the camp safe, about seven that evening, having only ten men wounded. Labienus too retreated to his camp, after having thoroughly fatigued his troops with the pursuit: in which, besides a great number wounded, his loss amounted to about three hundred men. And Scipio withdrew his legions and elephants, whom, for the greater terror, he had ranged before his camp within view of Caesar's army.

71

Caesar, to meet enemies of this sort, was necessitated to instruct his soldiers, not like a general of a veteran army which had been victorious in so many battles, but like a fencing master training up his gladiators, with what foot they must advance or retire; when they were to oppose and make good their ground; when to counterfeit an attack; at what place, and in what manner to launch their javelins. For the enemy's light-armed troops gave wonderful trouble and annoyance to our army; because they not only deterred the cavalry from the encounter, by killing their horses with their javelins, but likewise wearied out the legionary soldiers by their swiftness: for as often as these heavy-armed troops advanced to attack them, they evaded the danger by a quick retreat.

72

Caesar was rendered very anxious by these occurrences; because as often as he engaged with his cavalry, without being supported by the infantry, he found himself by no means a match for the enemy's horse, supported by their light-armed foot: and as he had no experience of the strength of their legions, he foresaw still greater difficulties when these should be united, as the shock must then be overwhelming. In addition to this, the number and size of the elephants greatly increased the terror of the soldiers; for which, however, he found a remedy, in causing some of those animals to be brought over from Italy, that his men might be accustomed to the sight of them, know their strength and courage, and in what part of the body they were most vulnerable. For as the elephants are covered with trappings and ornaments, it was necessary to inform them what parts of the body remained naked, that they might direct their darts thither. It was likewise needful to familiarize his horses to the cry, smell, and figure of these animals; in all of which he succeeded to a wonder; for the soldiers quickly came to touch them with their hands, and to be sensible of their tardiness; and the cavalry attacked them with blunted darts, and, by degrees, brought their horses to endure their presence.

73

For these reasons already mentioned, Caesar was very anxious, and proceeded with more slowness and circumspection than usual, abating considerably in his wonted expedition and celerity. Nor ought we to wonder; for in Gaul he had under him troops accustomed to fight in a champaign country, against an open undesigning enemy, who despised artifice, and valued themselves only on their bravery. But now he was to habituate his soldiers to the arts and contrivances of a crafty enemy, and teach them what to pursue, and what to avoid. The sooner therefore to instruct them in these matters, he took care not to confine his legions to one place, but under pretense of foraging, engaged them in frequent marches, and counter-marches; because he thought that the enemy's troops would not lose his track. Three days after, he drew up his forces with great skill, and marching past Scipio's camp, waited for him in an open plain; but seeing that he still declined a battle, he retreated to his camp a little before evening.

74

Meantime embassadors arrived from the town of Vacca, bordering upon Zeta, of which we have observed Caesar had possessed himself. They requested and entreated that he would send them a garrison, promising to furnish many of the necessaries of war. At the same time, by the will of the gods, and their kindness to Caesar, a deserter informed him, that Juba had, by a quick march, before Caesar's troops could arrive, reached the town and surrounded it, and after taking possession of it, massacred the inhabitants, and abandoned the place itself to the plunder of his soldiers.

75

Caesar, having reviewed his army the twelfth day before the calends of April, advanced next day, with all his forces, five miles beyond his camp, and remained a considerable time in order of battle, two miles from Scipio's. When he saw distinctly that the enemy, though frequently and for a long time challenged to a battle, declined it, he led back his troops. Next day he decamped, and directed his march toward Sarsura, where Scipio had a garrison of Numidians, and a magazine of corn. Labienus being informed of this motion, began to harass his rear with the cavalry and light-armed troops: and having made himself master of part of the baggage, was encouraged to attack the legions themselves, believing they would fall an easy prey, under the load and encumbrance of a march. However, this circumstance had not escaped Caesar's attention, for he had ordered three hundred men out of each legion to hold themselves in readiness for action. These being sent against Labienus, he was so terrified at their approach, that he shamefully took to flight, great numbers of his men being killed or wounded. The legionaries returned to their standards, and pursued their march. Labienus continued to follow us at a distance along the summit of the mountains on our right.

76

Caesar, arriving before Sarsura, took it in presence of the enemy, who durst not advance to its relief; and put to the sword the garrison which had been left there by Scipio, under the command of P. Cornelius, one of Scipio's veterans, who, after a vigorous defense, was surrounded slain. Having given all the corn in the place to the army, he marched next day to Tisdra, where Considius was, with a strong garrison and his cohort of gladiators. Caesar, having taken a view of the town, and being deterred from besieging it by want of corn, set out immediately, and after a march of four miles, encamped near a river. He marched from it on the fourth day, and then returned to his former camp at Agar. Scipio did the same, and retreated to his old quarters.

77

Meantime the inhabitants of Thabena, a nation situated on the extreme confines of Juba's kingdom, along the seacoast, and who had been accustomed to live in subjection to that monarch, having massacred the garrison left there by the king, sent deputies to Caesar to inform him of what they had done, and to beg he would take under his protection a city which deserved so well of the Roman people. Caesar, approving their conduct, sent M. Crispus the tribune, with a cohort, a party of archers, and a great number of engines of war, to charge himself with the defense of Thabena. At the same time the legionary soldiers, who, either on account of sickness or for other reasons, had not been able to come over into Africa with the rest, to the number of four thousand foot, four hundred horse, and a thousand archers and slingers, reached Caesar by one embarkation. With these and his former troops, he advanced into a plain eight miles distant from his own camp, and four from that of Scipio, where he awaited the enemy in order of battle.

78

There was a town below Scipio's camp, of the name of Tegea, where he had a garrison of four hundred horse. These he drew up on the right and left of the town; and bringing forth his legions, formed them in order of battle upon a hill somewhat lower than his camp, and which was about a thousand paces distant from it. After he had continued a considerable time in one place, without offering to make any attempt, Caesar sent some squadrons of horse, supported by his light-armed infantry, archers, and slingers, to charge the enemy's cavalry, who were on duty before the town. After Caesar's troops advanced and came to the charge with their horses at a gallop, Placidius began to extend his front, that he might at once surround us and give us a warm reception. Upon this Caesar detached three hundred legionaries to our assistance, while at the same time Labienus was continually sending fresh reinforcements, to replace those that were wounded or fatigued. Our cavalry, who were only four hundred in number, not being able to sustain the charge of four thousand, and being besides greatly harassed by the light-armed Numidians, began at last to give ground: which Caesar observing, detached the other wing to their assistance: who, joining those that were like to be overpowered, fell in a body upon the enemy, put them to flight, slew or wounded great numbers, pursued them three miles quite to the mountains, and then returned to their own men. Caesar continued in order of battle till four in the afternoon, and then retreated to his camp without the loss of a man. In this action

Placidius received a dangerous wound in the head, and had many of his best officers either killed or wounded.

79

After he found that he could not by any means induce the enemy to come down to the plain and make trial of the legions, and that he could not encamp nearer them for want of water, in consideration of which alone, and not from any confidence in their numbers, the Africans had dared to despise him; he decamped the day before the nones of April at midnight, marched sixteen miles beyond Agar to Thapsus, where Virgilius commanded with a strong garrison, and there fixed his camp, and began to surround the town the very day on which he arrived, and raised redoubts in proper places, as well for his own security, as to prevent any succors from entering the town. In the mean time, Scipio, on learning Caesar's designs, was reduced to the necessity of fighting, to avoid the disgrace of abandoning Virgilius and the Thapsitani, who had all along remained firm to his party; and therefore, following Caesar without delay, he posted himself in two camps eight miles from Thapsus.

80

Now there were some salt-pits, between which and the sea was a narrow pass of about fifteen hundred paces, by which Scipio endeavored to penetrate and carry succors to the inhabitants of Thapsus. But Caesar anticipating that this might happen, had the day before raised a very strong fort at the entrance of it, in which he left a triple garrison; and encamping with the rest of his troops in the form of a half moon, carried his works round the town. Scipio, disappointed in his design, passed the day and night following a little above the morass; but early next morning advanced within a small distance of the last mentioned camp and fort, where he began to intrench himself about fifteen hundred paces from the sea. Caesar being informed of this, drew off his men from the works; and leaving Asprenas the proconsul, with two legions, at the camp, marched all the rest of his forces with the utmost expedition to that place. He left part of the fleet before Thapsus, and ordered the rest to make as near the shore as possible toward the enemy's rear, observing the signal he should give them, upon which they were to raise a sudden shout, that the enemy, alarmed and disturbed by the noise behind them, might be forced to face about.

81

When Caesar came to the place, he found Scipio's army in order of battle before the intrenchments, the elephants posted on the right and left wings, and part of the soldiers busily employed in fortifying the camp. Upon sight of this disposition, he drew up his army in three lines, placed the tenth and second legions on the right wing, the eighth and ninth on the left, five legions in the center, covered his flanks with five cohorts, posted opposite the elephants, disposed the archers and slingers in the two wings, and intermingled the light-armed troops with his cavalry. He himself on foot went from rank to rank, to rouse the courage of the veterans, putting them in mind of their former victories, and animating them by his kind expressions. He exhorted the new levies who had never yet been in battle to emulate the bravery of the veterans, and endeavor by a victory to attain the same degree of fame, glory, and renown.

82

As he ran from rank to rank, he observed the enemy about the camp very uneasy, hurrying from place to place, at one time retiring behind the rampart, another coming out again in great tumult and confusion. As many others in the army began to observe this, his lieutenants and volunteers begged him to give the signal for battle, as the immortal gods promised him a decisive victory. While he hesitated and strove to repress their eagerness and desires, exclaiming that it was not his wish to commence the battle by a sudden sally, at the same time keeping back his army, on a sudden a trumpeter in the right wing, without Caesar's leave, but compelled by the soldiers, sounded a charge. Upon this all the cohorts began to rush toward the enemy, in spite of the endeavors of the centurions, who strove to restrain them by force, lest they should charge withal the general's order, but to no purpose.

83

Caesar perceiving that the ardor of his soldiers would admit of no restraint, giving "good fortune" for the word, spurred on his horse, and charged the enemy's front. On the right wing the archers and slingers poured their eager javelins without intermission upon the elephants, and by the noise of their slings and stones, so terrified these animals, that turning upon their own men, they trod them down in heaps, and rushed through the half-finished gates of the camp. At the same time the Mauritanian horse, who were in the same wing with the elephants, seeing themselves deprived of their assistance, betook themselves to flight. Whereupon the legions wheeling round the elephants, soon possessed themselves of the enemy's intrenchments, and some few that made great resistance being slain, the rest fled with all expedition to the camp they had quitted the day before.

84

And here we must not omit to notice the bravery of a veteran soldier of the fifth legion. For when an elephant which had been wounded in the left wing, and, roused to fury by the pain, ran against an unarmed sutler, threw him under his feet, and kneeling on him with his whole weight, and brandishing his uplifted trunk, with hideous cries, crushed him to death, the soldier could not refrain from attacking the animal. The elephant, seeing him advance with his javelin in his hand, quitted the dead body of the sutler, and seizing him with his trunk, wheeled him round in the air. But he, amid all the danger, preserving his presence of mind, ceased not with his sword to strike at the elephant's trunk, which enclasped him, and the animal, at last overcome with the pain, quitted the soldier, and fled to the rest with hideous cries,

85

Meanwhile the garrison of Thapsus, either designing to assist their friends, or abandoning the town to seek safety by flight, sallied out by the gate next the sea, and wading navel deep in the water; endeavored to reach the land. But the servants and attendants of the camp, attacking them with darts and stones, obliged them to return to the town. Scipio's forces meanwhile being beaten, and his men fleeing on all sides, the legions instantly began the pursuit, that they might have no time to rally. When they arrived at the camp to which they fled, and where, having repaired it, they hoped to defend themselves they began to think of choosing a commander, to whose, authority and orders they might submit; but finding none on whom they could rely, they threw down their arms, and fled to the king's quarter. Finding this, on their arrival, occupied by Caesar's forces, they retired to a hill, where, despairing of safety, they cast down their arms, and saluted them in a military manner. But this stood them in little stead, for the veterans, transported with rage and anger, not only could not be induced to spare the enemy, but even killed or wounded several citizens of distinction in their own army, whom they upbraided as authors of the war. Of this number was Tullius Rufus the quaestor, whom a soldier designedly ran through with a javelin; and Pompeius Rufus, who was wounded with a sword in the arm, and would doubtless have been slain, had he not speedily fled to Caesar for protection. This made several Roman knights and senators retire from the battle, lest the soldiers, who after so signal a victory assumed an unbounded license, should be induced by the hopes of impunity to wreck their fury on them likewise. In short all Scipio's soldiers, though they implored the protection of Caesar, were in the very sight of that general, and in spite of his entreaties to his men to spare them, without exception put to the sword.

86

Caesar, having made himself master of the enemy's three camps, killed ten thousand, and putting the rest to flight, retreated to his own quarters with the loss of not more than fifty men and a few wounded. In his way he appeared before the town of Thapsus, and ranged all the elephants he had taken in the battle, amounting to sixty-four, with their ornaments, trappings, and castles, in full view of the place. This he did in hopes that possibly Virgilius and those that were besieged with him might give over the idea of resistance on learning the defeat of their friends. He even called and invited him to submit, reminding him of his clemency and mildness; but no answer being given, he retired from before the town. Next day, after returning thanks to the gods, he assembled his army before Thapsus, praised his soldiers in presence of the inhabitants, rewarded the victorious, and from his tribunal extended his bounty to every one, according to their merit and services. Setting out thence immediately he left the proconsul C. Rebellius, with three legions, to continue the siege, and sent Cn. Domitius with two to invest Tisdra, where Considius commanded. Then ordering M. Messala to go before with the cavalry, he began his march to Utica.

87

Scipio's cavalry, who had escaped out of the battle, taking the road to Utica, arrived at Parada; but being refused admittance by the inhabitants, who heard of Caesar's victory, they forced the gates, lighted a great fire in the middle of the forum, and threw all the inhabitants into it, without distinction of age or sex, with their effects; avenging in this manner, by an unheard of cruelty, the affront they had received. Thence they marched directly to Utica. M. Cato, some time before, distrusting the inhabitants of that city, on account of the privileges granted them by the Julian law, had disarmed and expelled the populace, obliging them to dwell without the Warlike gate, in a small camp surrounded by a slight intrenchment, around which he had planted guards, while at the same time he put the senators under arrest. The cavalry attacked their camp, knowing them to be favorers of Caesar, and intending to wipe out by their destruction, the disgrace of their own defeat. But the people, animated by Caesar's victory, repulsed them with stones and clubs. They therefore threw themselves into the town, killed many of the inhabitants, and pillaged their houses. Cato, unable to prevail with them to abstain from rapine and slaughter, and undertake the defense of the town, as he was not ignorant of what they aimed at, gave each a hundred sesterces to make them quiet. Sylla Faustus did the same out of his own money; and marching with them from Utica, advanced into the kingdom.

88

A great many others that had escaped out of the battle, fled to Utica. These Cato assembled, with three hundred more who had furnished Scipio with money for carrying on the war, and exhorted them to set their slaves free, and in conjunction with them defend the town. But finding that though part assembled, the rest were terrified and determined to flee, he gave over the attempt, and furnished them with ships to facilitate their escape. He himself, having settled all his affairs with the utmost care, and commended his children to L. Caesar his quaestor, without the least indication which might give cause of suspicion, or any change in his countenance and behavior, privately carried a sword into his chamber when he retired to rest, and stabbed himself with it. When the wound not proving mortal, he fell heavily to the ground, his physician and friends suspecting what was going on, burst into the room and began to stanch and bind up his wound, he himself most resolutely tore it open, and met death with the greatest determination. The Uticans, though they hated his party, yet in consideration of his singular integrity, his behavior so different from that of the other chiefs, and because he had strengthened their town with wonderful fortifications, and increased the towers, interred him honorably. L. Caesar, that he might procure some advantage by his death, assembled the people, and after haranguing them, exhorted them to open their gates, and throw themselves upon Caesar's clemency, from which they had the greatest reason to hope the best. This advice being followed, he came forth to meet Caesar. Messala having reached Utica, according to his orders, placed guards at the gates.

89

Meanwhile Caesar, leaving Thapsus came to Usceta, where Scipio had laid up a great store of corn, arms, darts, and other warlike provisions, under a small guard. He soon made himself master of the place, and marched directly to Adrumetum, which he entered without opposition. He took an account of the arms, provisions, and money in the town; pardoned Q. Ligarius, and C. Considius; and leaving Livineius Regulus there with one legion, set out the same day for Utica. L. Caesar, meeting him by the way, threw himself at his feet, and only begged for his life. Caesar, according to his wonted clemency, easily pardoned him, as he did likewise Caecina, C. Ateius, P. Atrius, L. Cella, father and son, M. Eppius, M. Aquinius, Cato's son, and the children of Damasippus. He arrived at Utica in the evening by torch-light, and continued all that night without the town.

90

Early on the morning of the following day he entered the place, summoned an assembly of the people, and thanked them for the affection they had shown to his cause. At the same time he censured severely, and enlarged upon the crime of the Roman citizens and merchants, and the rest of the three hundred, who had furnished Scipio and Varus with money; but concluded with telling them, that they might show themselves without fear, as he was resolved to grant them their lives, and content himself with exposing their effects to sale; but that he would give them notice when their goods were to be sold, and the liberty of redeeming them upon payment of a certain fine. The merchants, half dead with fear, and conscious that they merited death, hearing upon what terms life was offered them, greedily accepted the condition, and entreated Caesar that he would impose a certain sum in gross upon all the three hundred. Accordingly, he amerced them in two hundred thousand sesterces, to be paid to the republic, at six equal payments, within the space of three years. They all accepted the condition, and considering that day as a second nativity, joyfully returned thanks to Caesar.

91

Meanwhile, king Juba, who had escaped from the battle with Petreius, hiding himself all day in the villages, and traveling only by night, arrived at last in Numidia. When he came to Zama, his ordinary place of residence, where were his wives and children, with all his treasures, and whatever he held most valuable, and which he had strongly fortified at the beginning of the war; the inhabitants, having heard of Caesar's victory, refused him admission, because, upon declaring war against the Romans, he had raised a mighty pile of wood in the middle of the forum, designing, if unsuccessful, to massacre all the citizens, fling their bodies and effects upon the pile, then setting fire to the mass, and throwing himself upon it, destroy all without exception, wives, children, citizens, and treasures, in one general conflagration. After continuing a considerable time before the gates, finding that neither threats nor entreaties would avail, he at last desired them to deliver up his wives and children, that he might carry them along with him. But receiving no answer, and seeing them determined to grant him nothing, he quitted the place, and retired to one of his country-seats with Petreius and a few horse.

92

Meantime the Zamians sent embassadors to Caesar at Utica, to inform him of what they had done, and to request "that he should send them aid before the king could collect an army and besiege them; that they were determined to defend the town for him as long as life remained." Caesar commended the embassadors, and sent them back to acquaint their fellow-citizens that he was coming himself to their relief. Accordingly, setting out the next day from Utica with his cavalry, he directed his march toward the kingdom. Many of the king's generals met him on the way, and sued for pardon; to all of whom a favorable hearing was given, and they attended him to Zama. The report of his clemency and mildness spreading into all parts, the whole Numidian cavalry flocked to him at Zama, and were there relieved from their fears.

93

During these transactions, Considius, who commanded at Tisdra, with his own retinue, a garrison of Getulians, and a company of gladiators, hearing of the defeat of his party, and terrified at the arrival of Domitius and his legions, abandoned the town; and privately withdrawing, with a few of the barbarians, and all his money, fled hastily toward the kingdom. The Getulians, to render themselves masters of his treasure, murdered him by the way, and fled every man where he could, Meantime, C. Virgilius, seeing himself shut up by sea and land, without the power of making a defense; his followers all slain or put to flight; M. Cato dead by his own hands at Utica; Juba despised and deserted by his own subjects; Sabura and his forces defeated by Sitius; Caesar received without opposition at Utica; and that of so vast an army, nothing remained capable of screening him or his children; thought it his most prudent course, to surrender himself and the city to the proconsul Caninius, by whom he was besieged.

94

At the same time king Juba, seeing himself excluded from all the cities of his kingdom, and that there remained no hopes of safety; having supped with Petreius, proposed an engagement, sword in hand, that they might die honorably. Juba, as being the stronger, easily got the better of his adversary, and laid him dead at his feet: but endeavoring afterward to run himself through the body, and wanting strength to accomplish it, he was obliged to have recourse to one of his slaves, and, by entreaties, prevailed upon him to put him to death.

95

In the mean time, P. Sitius, having defeated the army of Sabura, Juba's lieutenant, and slain the general, and marching with a few troops through Mauritania, to join Caesar, chanced to fall in with Faustus and

Afranius, who were at the head of the party that had plundered Utica, amounting in all to about fifteen hundred men, and designing to make the best of their way to Spain. Having expeditiously placed himself in ambuscade during the night, and attacking them by day-break, he either killed or made them all prisoners, except a few that escaped from the van. Afranius and Faustus were taken among the rest, with their wives and children: but some few days after, a mutiny arising among the soldiers, Faustus and Afranius were slain. Caesar pardoned Pompeia, the wife of Faustus, with her children, and permitted her the free enjoyment of all her effects.

96

Meanwhile Scipio, with Damasippus and Torquatus, and Plaetorius Rustianus, having embarked on board some galleys, with the intention of making for the coast of Spain; and being long and severely tossed by contrary winds, were at last obliged to put into the port of Hippo, where the fleet commanded by P. Sitius chanced at that time to be. Scipio's vessels, which were but small, and few in number, were easily surrounded and sunk, by the larger and more numerous ships of Sitius; on which occasion Scipio, and all those whom we have mentioned above, as having embarked with him, perished.

97

Meanwhile Caesar, having exposed the king's effects to public sale at Zama, and confiscated the estates of those who, though Roman citizens, had borne arms against the republic; after conferring rewards upon such of the Zamians as had adopted the design of excluding the king, he abolished all the royal tribunes, converted the kingdom into a province; and appointing Crispus Sallustius to take charge of it, with the title of proconsul, returned to Utica. There he sold the estates of the officers who had served under Juba and Petreius, fined the people of Thapsus twenty thousand sesterces, and the company of Roman merchants there thirty thousand; he likewise fined the inhabitants of Adrumetum in thirty thousand, and their company fifty thousand; but preserved the cities and their territories from insult and plunder. Those of Leptis, whom Juba had pillaged some time before, and who, upon complaint made to the senate by their deputies, had obtained arbitrators and restitution, were enjoined to pay yearly three hundred thousand pounds of oil; because from the beginning of the war, in consequence of a dissension among their chiefs, they had made an alliance with the king of Numidia, and supplied him with arms, soldiers, and money. The people of Tisdra, on account of their extreme poverty, were only condemned to pay annually a certain quantity of corn.

98

These things being settled, he embarked at Utica on the ides of June, and three days after arrived at Carales in Sardinia. Here he condemned the Sulcitani in a fine of one hundred thousand sesterces, for receiving and aiding Nasidius's fleet; and instead of a tenth which was their former assessment, ordered them now to pay an eighth to the public treasury. He likewise confiscated the estates of some who had been more active than the rest, and weighing from Carales on the third day before the calends of July, coasted along the shore, and after a voyage of twenty-eight days, during which he was several times obliged by contrary winds to put into port, arrived safe at Rome.

CÆSAR, GAIUS JULIUS (B.C.100-B.C.44). A famous Roman general, statesman, and writer; one of the most remarkable men of all time. He was the son of a Roman prætor of the same name, and was born July 12, B.C. 100. Two circumstances conspired to determine his sympathies in favor of democracy, and against a republican oligarchy. The first was the marriage of his aunt Julia with Gaius Marius; the second, the marriage of Cæsar himself, in B.C. 83, with Cornelia, daughter of L. Cinna, one of the principal enemies of Sulla. The anger of the dictator at this cost Cæsar his rank, property, and almost his life itself. Feeling that he would be safer abroad for a time, he went to Asia (B.C. 81); but on learning of the death of Sulla (B.C. 78), he hurried back to Rome, where he found the popular party in a state of great ferment, and anxious to regain what it had lost under the vigorous despotism of the aristocratic dictator. Cæsar, however, took no part in the attempts of Lepidus to overthrow the oligarchy; but he showed his political leanings by prosecuting (B.C. 77) Cn. Dolabella — a great partisan of Sulla — for extortion in his Province of Macedonia. To improve his eloquence, he went to Rhodes to study under the rhetor Apollonius Molo. In B.C. 74 he returned to Rome, where he had been elected pontifex, and now for the first time threw himself earnestly into public life. In the year B.C. 70 he attached himself to Pompeius, whose political actions at this time were of a decidedly democratic character. In B.C. 68 Cæsar obtained a quæstorship in Spain. On his return to Rome (B.C. 67) he married Pompeia, a relative of Pompeius, with whom he was daily becoming more intimate. In B.C. 65 he was elected to the curule ædileship, and lavished vast sums of money on games and public buildings, by which he increased his already great popularity. For the next few years Cæsar is found steadily skirmishing on the popular side. In B.C. 63 he was elected Pontifex Maximus, and shortly after prætor. During the same year occurred the famous debate on the Catiline conspiracy, in which the aristocratic party vainly endeavored to persuade the consul, Cicero, to include Cæsar in the list of conspirators. In B.C. 62 Pompeius returned from the East, and disbanded his army. Next year Cæsar obtained, as proprætor, the Province of Hispania Ulterior. His career in Spain was brilliant and decisive. On his return he was elected consul, along with M. Calpurnius Bibulus (B.C. 60). Cæsar, with rare tact and sagacity, reconciled the two most powerful men in Rome, who were then at variance — Pompeius and Crassus — and formed an alliance with them, known in history as the *First Triumvirate* (B.C. 60). Both of these distinguished men aided Cæsar in carrying his Agrarian Law (B.C. 59); and to strengthen still further the union which had been formed, Cæsar gave Pompeius his daughter, Julia, in marriage, though she had been promised to M. Brutus; while he himself married Calpurnia, daughter of L. Piso, his successor in the consulship. On the expiration of his term of office, he obtained for himself, by the popular vote, the Province of Gallia Cisalpina and Illyricum for five years, to which the Senate added — to prevent the popular assembly from doing so — the Province of Gallia Transalpina. Nothing could have been more favorable to Cæsar's aims. He had now an opportunity of developing his extraordinary military genius, and of gathering round him an army of veterans, whom perpetual victory should inspire with thorough soldierly fidelity and devotion to his person. This was the very thing he wanted to give him a reputation equal to that of his coadjutors, Pompeius and Crassus, whom, in genius, he far surpassed. Leaving, therefore, the political factions at Rome to exhaust themselves in petty strifes, Csesar, in B.C. 58, after the banishment of Cicero, repaired to his provinces, and during the next nine years conducted those splendid campaigns in Gaul by which, had he done nothing else, he would have "built himself an everlasting name." Cæsars first campaign was against the Helvetii, who were migrating from Switzerland into Gaul, and whom he totally defeated near Bibracte (Mont-Beuvray, near Autun). Out of 368,000 men, women, and children, only 110,000 remained. These were commanded by Cæsar to return home and cultivate their lands. The eyes of the Gauls were now turned upon the new conqueror, whose aid was solicited against an invader from beyond the Rhine, the German chief Ariovistus. Cæsar advanced against Ariovistus, who was utterly overthrown. And now Cæsar, having in the course of one campaign successfully concluded two important wars, led his troops into winter quarters.

Next year (B.C. 57) occurred the Belgic War, in which Cæsar successively routed the Suessiones, Bellovaci, Ambiani, and Nervii, who, alarmed at the progress of the Roman arms, had entered into an alliance with each other against the invaders. When the Senate received Cæsar's official dispatches, it decreed a thanksgiving of fifteen days — an honor never previously granted to any other general. During the winter and the spring following, Cæsar stayed at Lucca; and, after spending large sums of money in hospitality and for other less praiseworthy purposes, he departed for Gaul, where the flames of war had burst out in the northwest. The Veneti, a maritime people of Brittany, who possessed fleets of large vessels, were the chief instigators of the insurrection. Cæsar's plans were laid with consummate skill, and were crowned with the most splendid success. The Veneti were totally defeated, and most of the other Gallic tribes were either checked or subdued. Cæsar wintered in the country of the Aulerci and Lexovii (Normandy), having, in the course of three campaigns, conquered Gaul. Next year (B.C. 55) Crassus went to the East (where he was slain by the Parthians in B.C. 53), and Pompeius to Spain, while Cæsar's provincial government was prolonged for five years. He now undertook a fourth campaign against two German tribes who were about to enter Gaul. He was again successful; and, pursuing the fleeing enemy across the Rhine, which he had bridged, spent eighteen days in plundering the district inhabited by the Sigambri. He next invaded Britain, about the autumn; but after a brief stay in the island returned to Gaul. The Roman Senate, astonished at his hardihood and his successes in regions where no Roman army had ever been before, accorded him a public thanksgiving of twenty days. In B.C. 54 Ciesar opened his fifth campaign by a second invasion of Britain. On his return to Gaul, he was compelled — on account of the scarcity of corn, arising from drought — to winter his army in divisions. This naturally aroused the hopes of the Gauls, who thought the time had come for recovering their independence. An insurrection broke out in the northeast of Gaul, which was at first partially successful, but was ultimately crushed. Cæsar resolved to winter at Saniarobriva (Amiens), in the vicinity of the malcontents. In B.C. 53 he commenced his sixth campaign. It was chiefly occupied in crushing a second insurrection of the Gauls.

Cæsar then returned to northern Italy, that he might be able to communicate more easily and securely with his friends in Rome. That city was gradually becoming more anarchic, the evils of weak government more apparent; the hour for decisive action seemed to be approaching, and doubtless Cæsar's heart beat with expectation of the mighty future reserved for his boundless ambition, when all at once the prospect was darkened by a tremendous rebellion extending over the whole of Gaul, headed by a young warrior named Vercingetorix. It was in the dead of winter when the news came to Cæsar, who instantly saw that, at all hazards, he must preserve his fame and his army. Leaving, therefore, his rival Pompeius to succeed at Rome, he hurried to meet the insurgent hordes. His great difficulty was to collect his scattered legions. First crossing, with some Cisalpine and provincial troops, the mountains of Auvergne, though they lay six feet deep in snow, he suddenly appeared among the Arverni, who, terrified at his unexpected approach, sent for their chief, Vercingetorix, to come to their assistance. This was precisely what Cæsar wished. After some wonderful exhibitions of military skill and numerous successes by the Romans, Vercingetorix was shut up in Alesia (Alise in Burgundy), with all his infantry. Cæsar besieged him, and though harassed by nearly 300,000 Gauls without, who attempted, but in vain, to break through the well-defended Roman lines, he forced Vercingetorix to capitulate, many of the tribes now hastened to submit to Cæsar, who prudently determined to winter among the vanquished. The Senate voted him another public thanksgiving. In the next year (B.C. 51) Cæsar proceeded to quell the tribes who still held out. This he successfully accomplished, and having, in addition, reduced the whole of Aquitania, passed the winter of his eighth campaign at Nemetocenna, in Belgium, where he spent the time in a manner both politic and magnanimous. The Gallic princes were courteously and generously treated; the common people were spared the imposition of further taxes; and everything was done to render it possible for him to visit Italy with safety in the spring. This he did, and took up his residence at Ravenna, where he was informed of everything that was going on by the tribune C. Curio. There can be no doubt that at this moment he was the most popular man in the State, while his soldiery were devoted to him with a loyalty as enthusiastic as that which Bonaparte inspired when fresh from his Italian victories.

Meanwhile, Pompeius, whose vanity could not endure the greatness of Cæsar, had been gradually inclining again to the aristocracy, whose dread of the new conqueror was hourly increasing. After much futile diplomatic finesse on all sides, the Senate carried a motion "that Cæsar should disband his army by a certain day; and that if he did not do so he should be regarded as an enemy of the State." The tribunes Marcus Antonius and Q. Cassius put their veto on this motion; but they were violently driven out of the Senate chamber, and, fearing for their lives, they fled to Cæsar's camp. The Senate, in the madness of their terror, now declared war, and intrusted the conduct of it to Pompeius, whose pride in the invincibility of his military prowess hindered him from taking the necessary measures for the defense of the State. He fancied that his name would bring thousands to his standard, and he was even led to believe that Cæsar's troops were willing to desert their general; the result of which delusion was that when hostilities formally commenced, he had hardly any soldiers except two legions which had recently been in the service of his rival. Cæsar, on the other hand, perceiving that the time for decisive action had at length come, harangued his victorious troops, who were willing to follow him anywhere; crossed the Rubicon (a small stream which separated his province from Italy proper), and moved swiftly, amid the acclamations of the people, toward Rome. Pompeius fled to Brundisium, pursued by Cæsar, but contrived to reach Greece in safety, March 17, B.C. 49. The Italian cities had everywhere gladly opened their gates to the conqueror as a deliverer. Within three months Cæsar was master of all Italy.

Cæsar next subdued Pompeius's legates in Spain, who were at the head of considerable forces. On his return he took Massilia (Marseilles), where he learned that he had been appointed dictator of the Republic — a function which at this time he retained for only eleven days; but these were honorably distinguished by the passing of several humane enactments. Pompeius, now thoroughly alive to the magnitude of his danger, had gathered a powerful array in Egypt, Greece, and the East, while his fleet swept the sea. Cæsar, however, crossing the Adriatic at an unexpected season, hastened to Dyrrbachium, where Pompeius's stores were; but was nevertheless outstripped by his opponent. Pompeius intrenched his army upon some high ground near the city, where he was besieged by Cæsar. The first encounter was favorable to Pompeius, who drove back Cæsars legions with much loss. The latter now retreated to Thessaly, followed by his exulting enemies. A second battle ensued on the plains of Pharsalia, August 9, B.C. 48. Pompeius's army was utterly routed and Pompeius himself fled to Egypt, where he was treacherously murdered. See POMPEIUS.

No sooner had the news reached Rome than Cæsar was again appointed dictator for one year, and consul for five years. He was invested with tribunitial power for life, and with the right of holding all the magisterial comitia except those for the election of the plebeian tribunes. He did not, however, return to Rome after the battle of Pharsalia, but went to Egypt, then in a distracted condition on account of the disputes regarding the succession. Out of love for Cleopatra (who subsequently bore him a son), he entered upon the 'Alexandrine War,' in which he was successful, and which he brought to a close in March, B.C. 47. He next overthrew Pharnaces, King of Bosporus, son of Mithridates, near Zela, in Pontus, August 2d of the same year, and arrived in Rome in September. He was once more appointed dictator, and the property of Pompeius was confiscated and sold. Before the close of the year he had set out for Africa, where his campaign against the Pompeian generals, Scipio and Cato, was crowned with victory at the battle of Thapsus, April 6, B.C. 46. Cato committed suicide at Utica; and with such irresistible celerity was the work of subjugation carried on, that by the end of the summer Cæsar was again in Rome. Now occurred that display of noble and wise generosity which proves Cæsar to have been possessed of a great, magnanimous nature. He was not a man that could stoop to the vulgar atrocities of Marius or Sulla, and so he majestically declared that henceforth he had no enemies, and that he would make no difference between Pompeians and Cæsesarians. His victories in Gaul, Egypt, Pontus, and Africa were celebrated by four great triumphs, during which the whole Roman populace was feasted and fêted by the magnificent liberality of the dictator.

He now proceeded to check, by wholesale enactments, as far as in him lay, the social evils which had long flourished in the city. During the year B.C. 46, also, he conferred a benefit on Rome and on the world by the reformation of the calendar, which had been greatly abused by the Pontifical College for political purposes. In the meanwhile Pompeius's sons, Gneius and Sextus, were in arms in Spain. Cæsar overwhelmed their forces at Munda (B.C. 45). He now received the title of 'Father of his Country,' and also of *imperator*, was made dictator and *præfectus morum* for life, and consul for ten years; his person was declared sacred, and even divine; he obtained a bodyguard of knights and senators; his statue was placed in the temples; his portrait was struck on coins; the month Quintilis was called Julius in his honor; and on all public occasions he was permitted to wear the triumphal robe. He now proposed to make a digest of the whole Roman law for public use; to found libraries for the same purpose; to drain the Pontine marshes; to enlarge the harbor of Ostia; to dig a canal through the Isthmus of Corinth; and to quell the inroads of the barbarians on the eastern frontiers. But in the midst of these vast designs he was cut off by assassination, on the Ides (15th) of March, B.C. 44. The details of this crime — the greatest disaster that could have befallen the Roman world, as subsequent events made plain — are too familiar to require narration. It is sufficient to say that of the sixty aristocrats who were in the conspiracy, many had partaken of Cæsar's generosity, and all of his clemency. A few, like Brutus, out of a weak and formal conscientiousness, based on theory rather than insight, were probably shocked by Cæsar's desire to change the form of government into an hereditary monarchy; but most of them, like Cassius, were inspired by a jealous hatred of the dictator, and the base ambition of regaining power at all hazards.

Cæsar, who was 56 years of age when he was murdered, was of a noble and kingly presence, tall of stature, and possessing a countenance which, though pale and thin with thought, was always animated by the light of his black eyes. He was bald-headed (at least, in the latter part of his life), wore no beard; and though of a rather delicate constitution naturally, he ultimately attained to the most vigorous health. His besetting sin was sensuality; but without meaning to detract from the criminality of his conduct in this respect, it may be said that it was as much the sin of the times in which he lived as his own, and that the superlative grandeur of his position gave a prominence to his licentiousness which a more humble lot would have escaped. His intellect was marvelously versatile. In everything he excelled. He was not only the first general and statesman of his age, but he was — excepting Cicero — its greatest orator. As an historian he has never been surpassed, and rarely equaled in simplicity and vigor of style, and in the truthfulness with which he narrates events of which he was an eye-witness. He was, moreover, a mathematician, philologist, jurist, and architect, and always took great pleasure in literary society. Most of his writings have been lost, though their titles are preserved; yet we still possess his invaluable *Commentarii* (generally known as "Cæsar's Commentaries on the Gallic and Civil Wars"). The *editio princeps* was printed at Rome (1449). The best edition of his works is that of Dinter (Leipzig, 1890). Cæsar's life was formally written in ancient times by Suetonius and Plutarch. Consult, also: Delorme, *César et ses Contemporains*, etc. (Paris, 1868); Napoleon III., *Histoire de Jules César* (Paris, 1865-66); Stoffel, id., *La Guerre civile* {Paris, 1888); Froude, *Cæsar* (London, 1879); Dodge, "Cæsar," in *Great Captains Series* (Boston, 1892); and Fowler, *Julius Cæsar and the Foundation of the Roman Imperial System* (New York, 1892). On the Gallic campaigns, consult Holmes, *Cæsar's Conquest of Gaul* (London, 1899).

www.ingramcontent.com/pod-product-compliance
Lightning Source LLC
Chambersburg PA
CBHW070943120626
46546CB00004B/1538